JourneyThrough®

Joshua

30 Daily Insights by **David Sanford**

Journey Through Joshua
© 2019 by David Sanford
All rights reserved.

Our Daily Bread Publishing is affiliated
with Our Daily Bread Ministries.

Requests for permission to quote
from this book should be directed to:

Permissions Department
Our Daily Bread Publishing
P. O. Box 3566
Grand Rapids, MI 49501, USA

Or contact us by email at
permissionsdept@odb.org

Scriptures taken from Holy Bible, New International Version® Anglicized, NIV®
Copyright © 1973, 1978, 1984, 2011 by Biblica, Inc®. Used by permission.
All rights reserved worldwide.

All websites listed are accurate at the time of publication, but may change in the
future or cease to exist. The listing of the website references does not imply our
endorsement of the site's entire contents.

Design by Joshua Tan
Typeset by Haw Shing Yee

ISBN,978-1-913135-57-7

Printed in the United Kingdom
21 22 23 24 25 / 5 4 3 2 1

Foreword

As the new leader of Israel after Moses' death, Joshua had many compelling reasons to be afraid. He faced a daunting task of taking land from hostile enemies. As a good soldier, however, Joshua said "yes!" to the orders of his Commander to be strong, to be courageous, to know His Word, to obey His commands, to not be afraid, and to never forget that God was with him (Joshua 1:2–9).

When Joshua proceeded to conquer the promised land, it proved that all of God's great promises would come to pass. Near the end of his life, Joshua held out the same challenge to the Israelites: Be strong. Obey God's Word. And do not forget that the Lord is with you to fight for you (23:6–10). Joshua had the courage to obey the Lord God because he believed His promises wholeheartedly. In turn, he exhorted Israel to do the same; after all, they had seen God's promises come true, too.

If we find ourselves filled with fear, could it be because we have forgotten who God is and what He has promised (1 Peter 5:7–11)? Like Joshua, we need to continually draw on our abiding source of courage—not our own physical strength or mental abilities, but on the presence and promises of the Lord God. How good that you and I can be filled with courage daily because of the Lord's exceedingly great promises!

Throughout this book, "Lord" is spelt with small capitals, which refers to "YHWH". The Hebrew term YHWH is believed to derive from the root HWY, meaning "to be". The name suggests that God simply is the eternal "I AM" (see Exodus 3:14). Most of the time, both "Lord" and "God" appear together, emphasizing His greatness.

May the Lord God bless you richly,
David Sanford

We're glad you've decided to join us on a journey into a deeper relationship with Jesus Christ!

The *Journey Through* series is designed to help believers spend time with God in His Word, book by book. Each title is written by faithful Bible teachers to help you read, reflect and apply God's Word, a little bit at a time. It's a great accompaniment to read alongside the Bible, digging deeper into God's Word. We trust the meditation on God's Word will draw you into a closer relationship with Him through our Lord and Saviour, Jesus Christ.

How to use this resource

READ: After reading and reflecting on the Bible verses, use the explanatory notes to help you understand the Scriptures in fresh ways.

REFLECT: Use the questions to consider how you could respond to God and His Word, letting Him change you from the inside out.

RECORD: Jot down your thoughts and responses in the space provided to keep a diary of your journey with the Lord.

An Overview

Before he died, Moses commissioned Joshua to lead the Israelites into the promised land (Deuteronomy 31:7–8). Now, the LORD himself commissions Joshua with a series of remarkable promises (Joshua 1:1–9).

Strengthened by these promises, Joshua leads the Israelites across the Jordan (chapters 2–4), renews their covenant with the LORD (chapter 5), and overthrows more than 30 evil kingdoms that had occupied the promised land (chapters 6–12).

Having assigned land east of the Jordan River, Joshua begins the task of dividing the land west of the Jordan (chapters 13–21), but these efforts go awry when some tribes refuse to trust the LORD and obey Him. A civil war even nearly breaks out, but is narrowly averted (chapter 22).

One of Joshua's last tasks is to deliver farewell addresses to the Israelite leaders and people together (chapters 23–24). He exhorts them to remain true to the LORD, just as the LORD had remained true to them.

In the end, does Joshua fulfil God's purposes in his generation? Without a doubt, yes. Does God keep all His promises to Joshua? Again, yes. We can thank the LORD for His promise-keeping mercy, grace, and love for us!

Structure of Joshua

1:1–18	Joshua commissioned to lead
2:1–5:15	Preparations for conquest
6:1–12:24	Conquest of the promised land
13:1–21:45	Division of the promised land
22:1–34	Unity of 12 tribes reaffirmed
23:1–24:28	Joshua's farewell addresses
24:29–33	Joshua's death

Key Verse

But as for me and my household, we will serve the LORD. —Joshua 24:15

Day 1

Read Joshua 1:1–9

If the book of Joshua were a movie, the LORD God would be the executive producer, director, screenwriter, and lead actor. Without the LORD God, nothing happens.

This movie would probably be dedicated to the late Moses, who is named no less than 51 times. Joshua often describes Moses as "servant of the LORD" (for example, Joshua 1:13–15; 22:4–5). He also quotes from Moses repeatedly, directly or indirectly (for example, 1:12–15; 8:30–35; 13:8–33; 14:1–13; 22:1–5). This is not surprising, since Moses has left behind a number of sacred, inspired scrolls known as "the Book of the Law of Moses" (8:31; 23:6), or simply, "the law of Moses" (8:32; 22:5).

The best supporting actor? That would be Joshua (meaning "the LORD saves" in Hebrew), who is named 149 times. Assuming he was about the same age as Caleb when they were sent out to explore Canaan (Numbers 13:1–16), Joshua would be about 80 years old by the time we come to Joshua 1.

In these opening verses, the LORD God, Creator of heaven and earth, gives Joshua six specific orders (Joshua 1:7–9). This experience must have been awe-inspiring, for Joshua would remember them so well that near his death, he would reiterate some of them in his final exhortation to the Israelites (23:6–10).

The LORD God's six commands apply equally to us today. We know this because they reverberate through the rest of the Old Testament—and, more importantly, are echoed and exemplified by Jesus (which also means "the LORD saves" in Greek) and by His apostles. For example:

- *Be strong:* 1 Corinthians 16:13; Ephesians 6:10
- *Be courageous:* Mark 6:50; Acts 4:13; 1 Corinthians 16:13
- *Know God's Word:* Matthew 22:29; Romans 15:4; 2 Timothy 3:15–17
- *Obey God's commands:* John 15:10–17; James 1:22–25; 1 John 2:3–4
- *Do not be afraid:* Luke 5:10; Hebrews 13:6; 1 Peter 3:14
- *Do not be discouraged, God will be with you:* Matthew 28:20; John 14:16–17; Hebrews 13:5

Some of the commands that Joshua receives come with promises. We sometimes see the Bible as a book of the LORD God's commands. But let's not forget that it's a book of God's rich promises, too. Not surprisingly, the word "promise" will

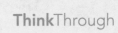

show up a dozen more times in the rest of the book of Joshua. In today's reading, God gives Joshua several specific promises. As we'll see in the coming days and weeks, each comes true!

Do you focus more on God's commands, or on His promises? How can you meditate on both, without neglecting either one?

What is one specific command from God that you need to keep today? What is one specific promise that will encourage and strengthen you?

Day 2

Read Joshua 1:10–18

As a good soldier, Joshua says "Yes!" to the orders of his Commander, the LORD God, and immediately issues instruction to the leaders of the two and a half tribes already settled on the east side of the Jordan River (Joshua 1:12–15). First, he instructs them to remember the word of the LORD, given through Moses (v. 13). Second, he reaffirms God's promises (v. 13). Third, he reiterates the LORD's command for them to help conquer the rest of the promised land (v. 14).

The book of Joshua records only half a dozen occasions when the Israelites speak to Joshua. This is the first such occasion. The leaders of the two-and-a-half eastern tribes pledge their loyalty to him (vv. 16–18).

In contrast, the book of Joshua records more than two dozen occasions when he speaks to the Israelites. The first such occasion also appears in today's Bible reading. The last such occasion appears shortly before his death.

Throughout the rest of the book, we will see Joshua speaking to:

- leaders of the 12 tribes of Israel (1:10–11; 22:1–8; 23:1–16)
- individuals (2:1; 7:19, 25; 14:13)
- all the people (3:5, 9–13; 4:21–24; 24:1–15, 19–20, 22–23; 24:25–28)
- the priests and Levites (3:6; 4:17; 6:6)
- small groups (4:4–7; 9:8, 22–23; 17:4–6; 18:8)
- his army (6:7, 10, 16–19; 8:3–8; 10:17–19, 22, 24–25, 27)

The order above is illustrative of Joshua's priorities. He talks to the leaders of the 12 tribes first (1:10–11), and the army last (6:7). **Unlike many military commanders, Joshua is not seeking to exalt himself and establish his power by gathering an army loyal to him. Instead, he remains focused on obeying his God wholeheartedly each and every day.**

Upon receiving God's mandate to lead the people, the first thing Joshua did was to talk to the leaders of the tribes to gather the people to get ready to cross the Jordan to "go in and take possession of the land the LORD your God is giving you for your own" (1:11). As we will see near the end of the book, Joshua finishes well. May you and I do the same!

Where do you typically hear others reiterate what the Bible teaches? Is there someone whom you could remind of God's Word, reaffirm His promises, or reiterate His commands to?

Reflect on your obedience to God's Word. In what ways are you similar or dissimilar to Joshua?

Day 3

Read Joshua 2:1–24

After finishing his address to the eastern tribes, Joshua secretly sends two trusted spies across the Jordan River. He sends them to one city—the city of Jericho. The Israelites were camped on the plains of Moab opposite Jericho, which is the first city they have to conquer in the promised land. Once inside the imposing walled city, the spies soon realise they are the most wanted men there. Humanly speaking, they are doomed!

But God provides them with an unexpected and surprising ally. **Rahab the prostitute couldn't have grown up in a more pagan culture, yet she expresses a remarkable faith in the Lord God (Joshua 2:9–11).** Do not miss her closing statement of faith: "For the Lord your God is God in heaven above and on the earth below." What remarkable faith, indeed!

So why does the Lord God command the destruction of all of Rahab's people? The answer is found in Genesis 15. The Lord had already made a promise to Abram to give the land of Canaan to his descendants, who would become a great nation and a blessing to all (Genesis 12:1–7). In Genesis 15:13–20, God told him that his descendants would be slaves in Egypt for 400 years (v. 13). Afterwards, "your descendants will come back here, for the sin of the Amorites has not yet reached its full measure" (v. 16). God's destruction of the Canaanites through the Israelites' conquest was His judgment upon them. It was His judgment for their horrific sins against Him and each other.

Who are these peoples whose horrific sins against their own families and neighbours regularly included incest, rape, violence, torture, and murder? They included the Hittites, Perizzites, Amorites, Canaanites, Girgashites, and Jebusites (vv. 19–21). Later, the Hivites were added to this list (Exodus 3:8, 17). The Lord had promised to drive out all these peoples (23:23; 33:2; 34:11) even though they were "seven nations larger and stronger than you" (Deuteronomy 7:1).

How cursed are these wicked people? After four centuries, they still have not repented. Instead, they have become evil through and through. Therefore, Moses says: "Completely destroy them—the Hittites, Amorites, Canaanites, Perizzites, Hivites and Jebusites—as the Lord your God has commanded you. Otherwise, they will teach you to follow all the detestable things they do in worshipping their gods, and you will sin against the LORD your God" (20:17–18).

In complete contrast with these peoples, Rahab turns to the LORD God of heaven and earth and trusts His purposes and protection for her family. What a great woman of faith, indeed.

ThinkThrough

Who can be a great woman or man of remarkable faith? How can you be one such person?

Our Holy God detests sin and the worship of other gods. How might today's reading change how you view sin and idolatry? How can you pray for yourself and others?

Day 4

Read Joshua 3:1–17

After hearing the report from the two spies, Joshua leads God's people across the Jordan River—a fierce, swollen torrent that threatens to drown them. Joshua assures them, however, that the LORD will perform a miracle (Joshua 3:5). After nearly 40 years at Moses' side, and having crossed the Red Sea on dry land, Joshua *knows* the LORD God can be trusted to keep His word—always!

True enough, God stops the flow of water, allowing the Israelites to cross over on dry land (vv. 15–17).

Humanly speaking, many of the things that occur in the book of Joshua would seem impossible. But Jesus reminds us: "What is impossible with man is possible with God" (Luke 18:27), for "With God all things are possible" (Matthew 19:26). These words echo statements made throughout the Old Testament, from "Is anything too hard for the LORD?" (Genesis 18:14) to "'It may seem marvellous to the remnant of this people at that time, but will it seem marvellous to me?' declares the LORD Almighty" (Zechariah 8:6).

These words shouldn't surprise us, because God is the same yesterday, today, and forever. He is almighty and nothing is too difficult for Him—during Joshua's time, during Jesus'

time, and in our time. With the LORD in charge, we can rest assured that He will make the way for His will to be done. Nothing is too hard for our omnipotent LORD God, who created the heavens and the earth with His word. He's the Almighty God, indeed!

What is Joshua's response? He shows an unflinching, wholehearted faith in God's power to carry out His promises. Our role as the LORD God's faithful followers, then, is not only to trust and obey Him, but also to encourage others to do the same, just as Joshua did.

All told, the LORD will speak directly to Joshua more than a dozen times through this book. As we continue our *Journey Through Joshua*, may we listen to the LORD as He speaks through His Word to our hearts. And may we trust and obey, and—like Joshua—encourage others to do the same.

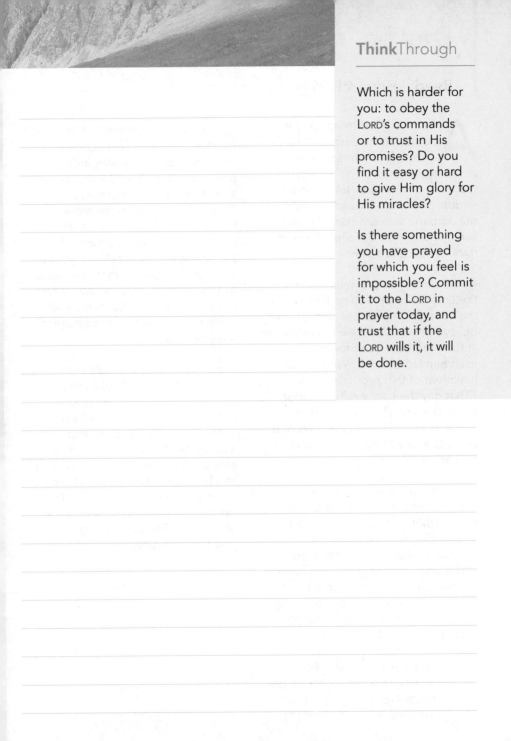

Which is harder for you: to obey the LORD's commands or to trust in His promises? Do you find it easy or hard to give Him glory for His miracles?

Is there something you have prayed for which you feel is impossible? Commit it to the LORD in prayer today, and trust that if the LORD wills it, it will be done.

Day 5

Read Joshua 4:1–24

After the Israelites cross the Jordan River, Joshua gives orders for them to set up an enduring memorial. The memorial, made up of 12 stones taken from the middle of the river, stands witness on the Jordan's western bank. No one can dispute what it means. A great miracle had taken place!

As we saw in the previous reading, the LORD God can do anything, even the humanly impossible. Joshua had believed in God's power unflinchingly; in turn, the LORD had promised to exalt him (Joshua 3:7). We see the fulfilment of that promise today: "That day the LORD exalted Joshua in the sight of all Israel; and they stood in awe of him all the days of his life, just as they had stood in awe of Moses" (4:14).

We must not make the mistake, however, of thinking that this book of the Bible is focusing on exalting Joshua (3:7; 4:14; 6:27). Instead, it is about exalting the LORD God and giving Him the glory, including through the use of memorial stones. Their purpose was to remind future generations about specific things God did for Israel (4:21–22).

The use of memorial stones recognised the need to keep remembering what the LORD God had done, and to keep giving Him honour, glory, and praise. Modern-day examples of "memorial stones" might include plaques by ponds and trees, as well as outdoor and indoor artwork. These plaques tell us the story behind the objects at hand, or who they have been dedicated to. They are not designed to tell everything; instead, they are meant to provoke questions so that we can tell others what the LORD God has done and invite them to join us in honouring and praising Him.

Imagine being in Joshua's shoes . . . trying to step into Moses' shoes. Each miracle by the LORD God reminds him to rely on God's power, not his own. The same principle is true today. If God calls you, He will enable you, even if it means stepping into big shoes. And let's find ways to commemorate the things that God has done through us so that those who come after us will continue to give God the glory.

What are some things the LORD has done for you? How can you commemorate them so that you and those after you will continue to give God the glory?

Does your church have any dedication plaques? If so, what do they commemorate?

Read Joshua 5:1–12

After Joshua dedicates the stone memorial, the Lᴏʀᴅ tells him that it is time for His people to renew their covenant with Him. This renewal takes place over the course of three deeply significant events: one, the circumcision of all males (Joshua 5:2–8); second, the celebration of Passover (v. 10); and third, the cessation of daily manna (v. 12).

The reasons aren't clear, but the Israelites had not circumcised any of their eight-day-old baby boys (see Genesis 17:9–14; Leviticus 12:3) since the nation's exodus from Egypt. Before the new generation attempts to conquer and take possession of the promised land—"a land flowing with milk and honey" (Joshua 5:6)—it is time to dedicate themselves to the Lᴏʀᴅ and His covenant.

In Genesis 17, the Lᴏʀᴅ makes a series of amazing promises to Abraham, and then commands him to be circumcised. This command applied to every male in his household then, and for all generations to come (vv. 10–13). Circumcision is a public sign that the Israelites are part of the Lᴏʀᴅ's covenant with Abraham. It also symbolises the cutting away of shame and guilt from the past (Joshua 5:9).

The Israelites had celebrated the Passover the day before they "marched out defiantly in full view of the Egyptians", led by Moses (Numbers 33:3). Exactly one year later, while still in the wilderness under Moses' leadership, they celebrated it again (9:1–14). Now, following the death of Moses and under Joshua's command, the Israelites celebrate the Passover right before beginning the conquest of the promised land (Joshua 5:10). May we, likewise, celebrate our salvation from sin and bondage, and remember that we are empowered to fulfil the Lᴏʀᴅ's purposes.

Joshua 5:11–12 tells us what happens next: "The day after the Passover, that very day, they ate some of the produce of the land: unleavened bread and roasted grain. The manna stopped the day after they ate this food from the land; there was no longer any manna for the Israelites, but that year they ate the produce of Canaan." For 40 long years, the miracle of manna had continued every day (Exodus 16:4–5). Now, it ceases as suddenly as it had begun, demonstrating that its provision was not a matter of chance, but of special, divine providence.

From now on, the Lᴏʀᴅ God will provide for them in another way. God had promised to bring Israel into a land of abundance, "a land with wheat and barley, vines and fig-trees, pomegranates, olive oil and honey" (Deuteronomy 8:8). Now, at last, they are tasting the fruit of the land and know that it is a foretaste of blessings to come!

ThinkThrough

In Exodus 16:4, the LORD promised "bread from heaven". In John 6:32–40, Jesus spoke of the "true bread of heaven" (v. 32) and himself as the "bread of life" (v. 35). What does that name say about Jesus? How should we therefore respond to Him?

Circumcision isn't just physical. In Deuteronomy 10:16 and 30:6, Jeremiah 4:4, and Romans 2:29, Moses, Jeremiah, and Paul speak about something more important. What is it and who does it?

Day 7

Read Joshua 5:13–15

After God's people renew their covenant with Him, Joshua has a dramatic encounter with the commander of the LORD's army. Some Bible scholars believe Joshua was actually in the presence of the pre-incarnate Jesus Christ!

The secret to Joshua's amazing faith and obedience is his willingness to listen intently whenever and however the LORD speaks to him. He immediately responds by asking: "What message does my Lord have for his servant?" (Joshua 5:14).

We have seen this in previous chapters, and we see it again today. Each time, Joshua comes away emboldened to trust the LORD God for celestial and terrestrial miracles. Tell the people to march around Jericho once a day for six consecutive days and then seven times on the seventh day? Tell the people to remain quiet until the moment to shout? Joshua obeys immediately, and becomes the catalyst for such "impossible" plans.

Some people claim to hear from God even when they do not; we don't want to trust such misguided persons. Others say that they have never heard from Him; we do not want to judge them. Still others hear God speak to them unmistakably. It may happen, as Joshua discovers, every few weeks or every few years. When it happens, the listeners know that God's message will be very specific, detailed, and often counterintuitive.

This is precisely Joshua's experience each time. Each time the LORD speaks to him, it is unmistakable. Even though many years may have passed, even though the LORD's commands sound counterintuitive, and even though the LORD's promises seem humanly impossible, there is no question in Joshua's heart. He *knows*, *trusts*, *believes*, and *immediately obeys*.

Do not wait for God to say something new. Instead, listen intently to what He has already said to you in the Scriptures. What has the LORD said to you during our journey so far through the book of Joshua? May He continue to nudge your heart and quicken your mind in the coming days!

How have you been listening to God? How can you learn from Joshua's example and habit of asking: "What message does my Lord have for his servant?" (Joshua 5:14).

Romans 15:4 tells us why God gave us His Word. Has this been your experience so far during our *Journey Through Joshua*? If so, in what ways?

Day 8

Joshua unquestioningly accepts the LORD's orders and does exactly what He commands. What great faith! God promises that Jericho's impregnable walls will collapse at His command—and they do, without harming the Israelites encircling it (Joshua 6:20).

This is amazing, considering what was involved. Excavations of Jericho have revealed that the city's fortifications featured a stone wall some 4 metres high. At its top was a smooth stone slope that angled upward at 35 degrees for 10 metres, where it joined massive stone walls that towered even higher.

But what's even more amazing is what archaeologists have found in the extensive layers of ruins and remains of Jericho, considered to be one of the world's oldest cities. One layer shows the collapsed walls around the city—except for one spot. There, in the early 1900s, two archaeologists discovered what appeared to be Rahab's house and several next to it.

This is especially significant, as we shall soon see. Joshua 6:25 tells us that "Joshua spared Rahab the prostitute, with her family and all who belonged to her, because she hid the men Joshua had sent as spies to Jericho—and she lives among the Israelites to this day." Spared the fate that befalls her city, Rahab turns away from worshipping idols to follow God, and becomes a part of God's people. Later, she would marry a Jewish husband, Salmon, and have a righteous son, Boaz—who would in turn become the ancestor of David and, ultimately, Jesus (see Ruth 4:21–22; Matthew 1:5, 16).

How good that the LORD gladly saves us, no matter our nationality, family background, or our past. What's more, how good that God rewards the faith of all who earnestly seek Him (Hebrews 11:6).

How good are the LORD's rewards? In this case, Rahab's unswerving faith in the one true God (Hebrews 11:31; James 2:25) not only gives her a place of honour as the great great-grandmother of King David, but also a distinguished place of honour in the genealogy of Jesus Christ. What good rewards, indeed!

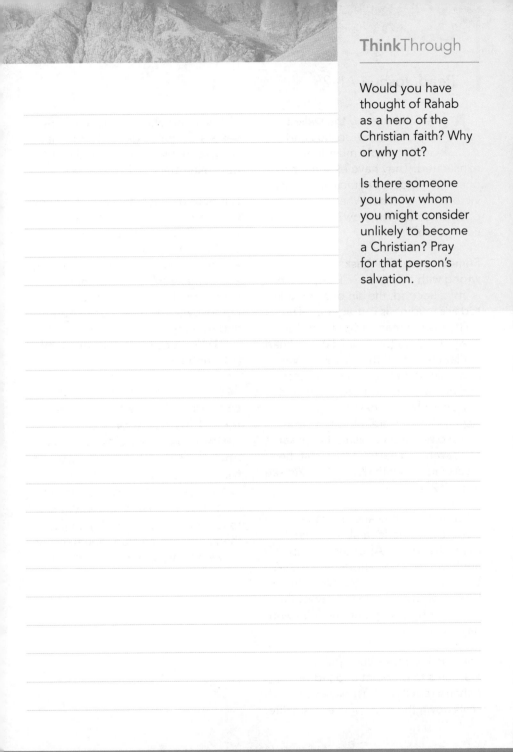

Would you have thought of Rahab as a hero of the Christian faith? Why or why not?

Is there someone you know whom you might consider unlikely to become a Christian? Pray for that person's salvation.

Day 9

Read Joshua 7:1–26

After conquering the walled city of Jericho, Joshua and God's people must feel exhilarated. They have experienced one of the most spectacular military victories of all time. What could possibly stop them now? The answer lies in a word: sin.

Some people might ask: "What's wrong with a little sin?" First, no sin is little. Second, the sin described in today's reading is outrageous. The guilty man, Achan, steals from the LORD's treasury (Joshua 7:11). God had earlier instructed that "all the silver and gold and the articles of bronze and iron are sacred to the LORD and must go into his treasury" (6:19). Achan's actions are a form of high-handed rebellion against the maker of heaven and earth. As a result, he incurs God's wrath (7:1, 10–12, 26; see also 22:20).

Of course, Joshua and the other leaders have no idea about what Achan has done. After they mourn until evening (7:6), and after Joshua's brief but heartfelt prayer (vv. 7–9), the LORD explains how He will reveal the covenant-breaking man the following day (vv. 10–15).

That the LORD took such public measures to pinpoint and judge Achan's rebellion must have sent chills down the back of every Israelite.

The warning of Moses, given many years ago, still rings true: "You may be sure that your sin will find you out" (Numbers 32:23).

Is it possible for Christians who know Christ's sacrifice on the cross to commit flagrant sins against the LORD, too? Yes, as we see in the example of Ananias and Sapphira in Acts 5:1–11, and in many others documented in the epistles. Such actions, if not followed by deep confession and true repentance, can lead to weakness, sickness, and even death (1 Corinthians 11:30).

Jesus didn't die for some of our sins. He died for them all, including the worst and most rebellious attitudes, words, and actions. But that doesn't mean the LORD doesn't care what we do anymore. In fact, it is just the opposite. We need to identify our sins, deeply confess them, and exhibit true repentance in how we think, speak, and behave.

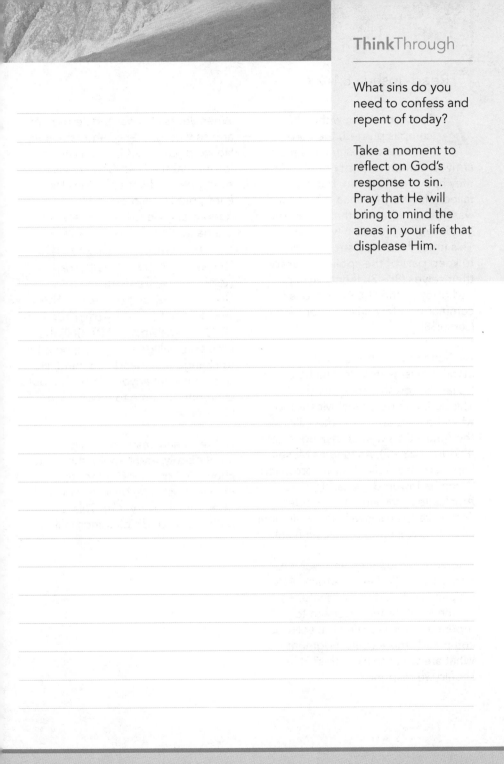

What sins do you need to confess and repent of today?

Take a moment to reflect on God's response to sin. Pray that He will bring to mind the areas in your life that displease Him.

Read Joshua 8:1–29

After Achan's sin within the camp is purged, the LORD commands Joshua and his army to conquer the city of Ai. Earlier, they had tried to do so, but had failed miserably (Joshua 7:3–5). God was not with them in that first battle because of Achan's sin (vv. 11–12). This time, the LORD instructs them to keep part of the spoils of war for themselves (8:1–2). If only Achan had obeyed the LORD's previous commands a few days earlier (see 6:18)!

As the men of Ai try to counter-attack the Israelites, Joshua holds out his javelin towards their city (8:18). This action mirrors what Moses did when he held up his hands while the Amalekites were attacking Israel (Exodus 17:8–12). As long as Moses kept his hands raised, Israel prevailed. When he lowered his hands, the Amalekites prevailed. No wonder Joshua keeps his javelin in the air until all of Ai is obliterated (Joshua 8:26).

A total of 12,000 men and women from Ai are killed in the attack. After waiting for decades and centuries for the inhabitants in Canaan to repent and turn to Him, the LORD God commands this earthly judgment. What are we to think of this? How should we respond?

When Jesus approached Jerusalem and saw its ignorance and rebellion, He wept (Luke 19:41). Let us not forget that the LORD God knows *everyone*. And not only does He *know*, but He also *cares*. He cares deeply, and He loves infinitely and eternally. **Yet, if anyone rebels against Him and flagrantly breaks His commandments (which are designed for humanity's protection), they will have to face judgment (2 Corinthians 5:10).** Still, the LORD God will do everything possible to change their heart and mind: He does not want anyone to perish, but everyone to come to repentance (2 Peter 3:9).

Unlike Achan, may we readily, immediately, and happily choose to know the LORD our God, to repent of our sin, trust Him, believe Him, and obey Him at every turn. *This* is the pathway to God's blessings in life.

ThinkThrough

Have you ever wept over the death of a loved one or friend who died without knowing Jesus? How do you think the LORD responded to your grief (see John 11:35)?

Read Romans 2:4–8. Why do some disobey the LORD knowingly and intentionally? How does it make you feel?

Day 11

Read Joshua 8:30–35

After the great victory over the city of Ai, Joshua renews Israel's covenant with the LORD. What he does was commanded by the LORD through Moses (Deuteronomy 11:29–30; 27:1–26. See also 28:1–68; 29:1–29; 30:1–20).

First, Joshua builds an altar for the LORD on Mount Ebal, where he was to proclaim the curses (Joshua 8:30–31; see Deuteronomy 11:29).

Second, he writes a copy of the Law of Moses, taking care to write down every word (Joshua 8:32, 34; see Deuteronomy 27:3, 8). This includes the Ten Commandments (Exodus 20:1–17, Deuteronomy 5:6–21).

Third, he has the ark of the covenant of the LORD placed between the two mountains (Joshua 8:33, one of the Bible's longest verses).

Fourth, Joshua calls the leaders and all of God's people to gather—half at Mount Gerizim and the other half at Mount Ebal, which is located at Shechem. The tribes of Reuben, Gad, Asher, Zebulun, Dan, and Naphtali stand on Mount Ebal, which stands to the north (see Deuteronomy 27:13), and the tribes of Simeon, Levi, Judah, Issachar, Joseph, and Benjamin stand on Mount Gerizim, to the south (v. 12).

Shechem is an area full of patriarchal history. It was at Shechem, that Abraham and Jacob—the father of Israel's 12 tribes—built an altar (Genesis 12:6–7; 33:18–20). In a sense, standing at Shechem was coming "home". It was also at Shechem, that Jacob exhorted his family to rid themselves of foreign idols (35:2–4) and suffered terrible tragedies involving his children (Genesis 34, 37). It was a place that spoke of real-life blessings and curses on the earliest Israelites. What a fitting location, indeed!

Then, Joshua reads the blessings and curses prescribed by the LORD and His servant Moses, making sure to read out every word to the people (Joshua 8:34).

Under the New Covenant, Christians are not under the old covenant curses, for we are forgiven and redeemed through Christ's sacrifice (Ephesians 1:7). "Praise be to the God and Father of our LORD Jesus Christ, who has blessed us in the heavenly realms with every spiritual blessing in Christ" (v. 3). Amen!

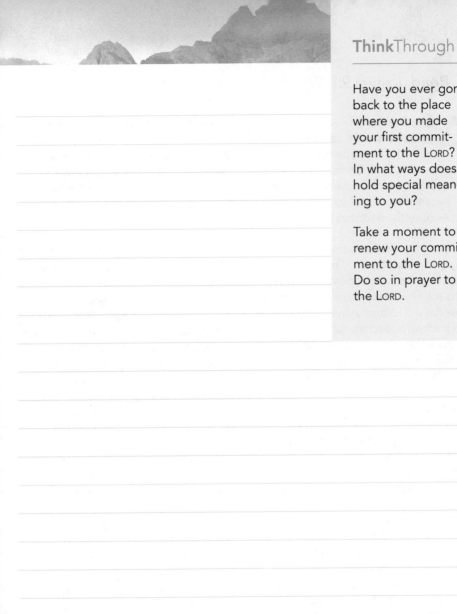

Have you ever gone back to the place where you made your first commitment to the LORD? In what ways does it hold special meaning to you?

Take a moment to renew your commitment to the LORD. Do so in prayer to the LORD.

Day 12

Read Joshua 9:1–27

After Joshua renews and reviews Israel's covenant with the LORD, he wrongly assumes all is well. Because of that assumption, he makes a colossal error and—despite his zeal to obey the LORD—directly disobeys Him.

Sadly, men of action sometimes see prayer as a last resort. Throughout Scripture, the LORD repeatedly invites us to ask Him for wisdom (for example, Proverbs 2:3–6 and James 1:5). Joshua and his fellow leaders, however, are deceived by what they see. They see the Gibeonites' "worn and patched sandals" and "dry and mouldy" bread (Joshua 9:5), and trust their words that they come from a distant country. Joshua and his leaders fail to pray before making a peace treaty with them (v. 14). Thankfully, Joshua will learn his lesson—just in time to ask for a great miracle in the next chapter.

Interestingly, the envoys from the large and feared city of Gibeon express great faith. When asked why they had deceived the Israelites, they tell Joshua: "Your servants were clearly told how the LORD your God had commanded his servant Moses to give you the whole land and to wipe out all its inhabitants from before you. So we feared for our lives because of you, and that is why we did this" (v. 24).

The Israelite leaders' response is also notable: "Let them live, but let them be woodcutters and water-carriers in the service of the whole assembly" (v. 21). Despite the deceit, the leaders decide to keep their promise to the Gibeonites.

This illustrates an important principle: **wisdom is needed to know how to obey the LORD's commands when we face a dilemma or conflicting laws.** Rahab had chosen to commit treason against her own city and bear false witness in order to protect the two Israelite spies (2:4–6) because she feared the God of the Israelites and acknowledged His sovereignty. Now, even though Joshua and his fellow leaders are supposed to wipe out all the inhabitants of Canaan, they decide to keep their promise to the Gibeonites. This agreement is sacred because it had been ratified by an oath made in the name of the LORD (9:15, 18–19). In keeping this promise, Joshua and the leaders show that they are men of integrity, men who stand by their word. Though humiliated by what had transpired, they do not want to bring disgrace on God and His people by breaking a sacred treaty.

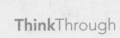

Today, let us not repeat the mistake of not enquiring of the LORD before making a decision (v. 14). Instead, let us ask the LORD for wisdom in every sphere of our lives.

Have you ever faced a dilemma of conflicting laws or commands? What were they, and how did you resolve the dilemma?

When did you last ask the LORD for wisdom? How did the LORD answer you?

Read Joshua 10:1–43

After the Gibeonites deceive Joshua into making a treaty with them, an alliance of southern kingdoms forms, attacks Israel, and is destroyed. Like Ai, they strike Israel as hard as they can. Unlike Ai, they do not wait for Joshua and his army to come to them. Instead, they go on the offensive and attack first.

Don't miss the fury and fullness of this brief sketch about a long string of stunning military victories (Joshua 10:40–42). What's more, don't miss the reference to the victorious Israelites putting their enemies under their feet (v. 24), which offers us a vivid picture of the Messiah's ultimate victory over all (Psalm 110:1; Matthew 22:44; Mark 12:36; 1 Corinthians 15:25–27; Ephesians 1:20–22). In the end, everything everywhere will be in complete subjection to the Lord.

Some sceptics and critics protest that the Lord should not have commanded Israel to wipe out all these men, women, children, and animals. Do their assertions have any merit? No. First, these peoples had waged wars against each other for centuries. Second, their religions were heinous, often involving sexual slavery and human sacrifices. Third, they had spurned the Lord and tested His patience generation after generation; instead of repenting, they had become even more wicked (see Day 3). If only they had repented!

Therefore, the Lord orders the complete destruction of the Hittites, Amorites, Canaanites, Perizzites, Hivites, Girgashites, and Jebusites, with the exception of the repentant Rahab and her family, and the believing Gibeonites.

Tragically, the Israelites do not obey the Lord fully, too, as we will see in subsequent chapters of Joshua. They will embrace wicked practices and idol worship, and tribe will fight against tribe for centuries. In the end, Israel's apostasy will split the nation into two kingdoms, both of whom will be conquered and deported to foreign lands.

Again, don't miss Joshua's amazing prayer in Joshua 10:12: "Sun, stand still over Gibeon, and you, moon, over the Valley of Aijalon", and the Lord's spectacular miracles in verses 13–14: "The sun stopped in the middle of the sky and delayed going down about a full day. There has never been a day like it before or since, a day when the Lord listened to a human being. Surely the Lord was fighting for Israel!"

Like Joshua, the righteous person who obeys the Lord

wholeheartedly eventually receives supernatural answers to prayer (James 5:16–18). May you and I know this experientially for the rest of our days.

Have you ever received a supernatural answer to prayer? What is something you need to bring before God in prayer, trusting in His might and love to answer you?

Finish this prayer: "LORD, when it comes to knowing, loving, trusting, and obeying You, I want to be nothing less than wholehearted. Help me to obey you in . . ."

Day 14

Read Joshua 11:1–15

After the alliance of southern kingdoms attacks Israel and is destroyed, an alliance of northern kingdoms forms, attacks Israel, and is obliterated (Joshua 11:1–8). Then comes a much longer campaign (v. 18) to obliterate each of their cities. This could have taken up to seven years.

As we saw in chapter 10, the book of Joshua is full of references to cities and kingdoms. So, what's up with all these places? The lists serve four distinct purposes: first, they list whom the Israelites conquer; second, they describe where Joshua meets his army for the next battle; third, they describe which regions and cities the Israelite tribes, clans, and families are to inherit and finish conquering; and fourth, they describe where Joshua meets the Israelite leaders and tribes for solemn assemblies.

The book of Joshua is full of great stories of faith. They include those of Rahab hiding the two spies, Israel crossing the Jordan River on dry ground, the miraculous conquest of Jericho, the conquest of Ai, the deception of the Gibeonites, and the miraculous conquests of the united armies of the southern kingdoms and later, the northern kingdoms.

More great stories of faith lie ahead! In addition, we will encounter lengthy descriptions of the territories assigned to each tribe. While the boundaries and cities might not appear to mean much to some of us today, they hold the seeds of dozens and dozens of future stories in Judges, Ruth, 1 and 2 Samuel, and the rest of the Bible. More importantly, these territorial assignments mean the world to Abraham, Isaac, and Jacob's descendants. Just as He promised, the LORD is blessing them with "a land flowing with milk and honey" (Exodus 3:8; Leviticus 20:24; Numbers 14:8; Deuteronomy 6:3; Joshua 5:6). Each territorial assignment is cause for much celebration.

Our lives may not be as exciting today; most of our days are probably routine. Yet each and every day is important to our well-being and our future. **When the LORD blesses us with new experiences of His wonderful providence, it is cause for praise.** We are to praise the LORD every ordinary day and seek to walk with Him faithfully as Joshua did (Joshua 11:15).

Think over what has happened in the past seven days. What can you thank God for? How can you make gratitude part of your thoughts and speech?

Finish this prayer: "LORD, I want to obey You and walk with You faithfully. Please . . ."

Day 15

Read Joshua 11:16–12:24

Obeying God's orders, Moses had conquered two vast kingdoms east of the Jordan River (Joshua 12:1–6). Now, Joshua has conquered a much larger area and its 31 wicked, pagan peoples west of the river (vv. 7–24). The reason is clear: "For it was the LORD himself who hardened their hearts to wage war against Israel, so that he might destroy them totally, exterminating them without mercy, as the LORD had commanded Moses" (11:20).

In giving this command, of course, the LORD was not being ruthless or maniacal. God does not want anyone to perish, but all to come to repentance (2 Peter 3:9). In Ezekiel 18:23, we read: "Do I take any pleasure in the death of the wicked? declares the Sovereign LORD. Rather, am I not pleased when they turn from their ways and live?"

While conquering the promised land, Joshua obeys the LORD's commands and proves that all of God's promises will come to pass. By now, Joshua may be 85 years old. Yet his love, trust, and obedience in the LORD God are as strong as ever. As a result, "Joshua took the entire land, just as the LORD had directed Moses, and he gave it as an inheritance to Israel according to their tribal divisions. Then the land had rest from war" (Joshua 11:23).

Be sure to note the key words, "inheritance", "land", and "rest". These three terms are found throughout the book of Joshua. Land given is not the same as land accepted, taken, and claimed. Just like when a cheque is given, unless it is accepted, banked in, and reflected in the bank account statement, it remains merely a gift. This major theme runs throughout the rest of the book of Joshua, becomes the main theme of the book of Judges, continues throughout the Old Testament, and forms the backdrop of several New Testament passages. It features in Hebrews 10:35–39 and also in all of Hebrews 4, which reminds us to "be careful that none of you be found to have fallen short of [his rest]" (v. 1). Verse 11 stresses that this gift of God's rest needs to be claimed: "Let us, therefore, make every effort to enter that rest, so that no one will perish by following their example of disobedience."

How good and essential it is for us to accept, take, and *claim* God's great promises.

Yet I can imagine the apostles, like the Old Testament writers before them, shaking their heads when they see people's response. When the LORD God promises us so much, why would anyone be content to accept so little?

Do you know any godly individuals who continue to show great faith in their age? What can you learn from them?

Finish this prayer: "LORD, Your answers to my specific prayers increase my faith and trust in You. Thank you for . . ."

Day 16

Read Joshua 13:1–7

After Joshua's conquests are tallied up, the Lord tells him that there is more territory within the promised land that needs to be conquered and divided among the tribes. This new campaign may have taken another five or ten years.

At this juncture, it is appropriate for us to pause and look at four questions that we may have asked as we read the accounts.

One frequently-asked question about the book of Joshua is: "Did these events really take place?" The answer is a resounding "Yes!" In fact, among the books of the Bible, the book of Joshua is one of the most thoroughly reviewed by the archaeological community. Archaeologists have discovered the city of Jericho—the first city the Israelites attacked and conquered upon entering the promised land—and noted that its location would have made it the first city the Israelites would have needed to conquer after crossing the Jordan River.

The second question is: "Did God really order the obliteration of the people in all these cities and kingdoms?" Yes, He did. But let's not forget that the people of Jericho were not given several minutes or hours to repent. And nor were the people of neighbouring cities and kingdoms given several days or weeks to repent. Rather, they were given many years and decades. Some were given centuries. "The Lord is patient" is an understatement of immense proportions.

The third question is: "How could an all-powerful and loving God wipe them all out?" Precisely because the Lord God is all-powerful and loving . . . and much more. **Though we may have difficulty reconciling God's actions with His character, we must always trust that God's actions is always consistent with His character. He is infinitely and eternally sovereign, holy, and loving.** As finite creatures, we will always find it difficult to fully comprehend His infinite mercy, grace, and forgiveness, even with the Bible in hand. But we can always trust that God will mete out His justice and mercy perfectly.

The fourth question is: "How can God be so heartless?" Again, let's always remember that the Lord God does not want anyone to perish, but all to come to repentance (2 Peter 3:9). This important truth reverberates through the Scriptures from Genesis to Malachi. It then reaches its crescendo in the Gospels.

The infinite anguish that Jesus felt in the hours, minutes, and seconds before He gave His life for the lost world eloquently answers, once and for all, any doubts about His ultimate goodness, rightness, mercy, and justice.

Which of these four questions have troubled you in the past or more recently?

Which of these questions still troubles you? Why? How will looking to Jesus and His sacrifice help you resolve these doubts?

Read Joshua 13:8–14:5

After hearing from the LORD, Joshua reaffirms the territorial assignments that Moses had made east of the Jordan River (Joshua 13:8–33). He does so before apportioning the lands to the west, so as to reassure them of their rightful inheritance.

Such reassurances are well deserved. Joshua will later applaud the military men from these eastern tribes for serving with courage, steadfastness, and valour to help their fellow Israelites conquer their share of the promised land (22:1–5).

Yet, in the rest of biblical history, no prominent judge, prophet, or ruler will ever arise from these two-and-a-half tribes; with perhaps the exception of Elijah from Tishbe in Gilead. This is not surprising in the case of Reuben (see Jacob's curse in Genesis 49:3–4), but it is in the case of Gad (see Moses' blessing in Deuteronomy 33:20). It's also surprising in the case of East Manasseh (compared with West Manasseh's heroes of the faith). The LORD wants to raise up godly leaders among all groups of His people everywhere. When it happens, it's cause for rejoicing. When it doesn't happen after years and decades, it's cause for concern.

Joshua 13:13 offers sober news: "But the Israelites did not drive out the people of Geshur and Maakah, so they continue to live among the Israelites to this day." We hear this indictment again four more times in 15:63, 16:10, 17:12–13, and 17:16–18. **Without godly leaders, people often stop trusting the LORD, obeying Him, and claiming His promised blessings.** That's exactly what we see here. Tribe after tribe refuses to trust the LORD and drive out the remaining hostile inhabitants within their territories.

Joshua 13:14 and 13:33 give what sounds like more sober news. Actually, it is the best of news: the tribe of Levi is not given a territory of their own because the LORD, and the sacred food offerings presented to Him, are "their inheritance, as he promised them" (v. 33). We see this again in 14:3–4 and 18:7. This does not mean they will not have places to live. In fact, it's just the opposite. As we will see later, the Levites are given an average of four cities with each of the other tribes. What blessings, both to Levi and the rest of Israel!

The question of places to live will come up again, when six women of faith—Caleb's daughter Aksah and Zelophehad's daughters Mahlah, Noah, Hoglah, Milkah, and Tirzah secure property that blesses their families for generations and centuries to come. Like them, women of faith today can rest assured that the LORD God wants to bless them, too!

Do you find it easy or hard to trust the LORD's promises to every believer today? Why?

Which of the LORD's promises give you the greatest comfort and hope? Why?

Day 18

Read Joshua 14:6–15:63

Starting with the tribe of Judah, Joshua begins to apportion lands to the remaining Israelite tribes. In contrast to all the other tribes, Judah produces a plethora of biblical villains and heroes.

One of the heroes at the time was Caleb, Judah's greatest hero. Caleb has stood shoulder to shoulder with Joshua, without fail, for many decades. Like Joshua, Caleb takes the LORD God's promises to heart and trusts they will be fulfilled in due time (Joshua 14:10, 12). In addition, like Moses, Caleb is the epitome of a brave and biblical, godly and gracious, valiant and victorious man of God. He "followed the LORD [his] God wholeheartedly" (vv. 8–9, 14). **Like Caleb, the righteous person today who obeys the LORD wholeheartedly eventually succeeds in extraordinary ways, with "the LORD helping" them (v. 12).**

In today's Scripture passage, we find not one but two stories about Caleb and his family's inheritance of land. In the first, Joshua gives Caleb the land that the LORD God promised to him and his family (vv. 13–14). In the second, Caleb gives his daughter Aksah a greatly appreciated second parcel of land (15:19–20).

The book of Joshua records only half a dozen occasions when people spoke to him. This is one such occasion (14:6–12). Notice that Caleb does not come alone; he comes with a delegation of top leaders within his tribe, who stand in full support and agreement with everything Caleb says (v. 6). It is important for Caleb to make his request publicly. That way, he avoids any appearance of asking Joshua for a personal favour. Also, he asks only for what the LORD God has promised would be "[his] inheritance and that of [his] children" (v. 9).

Notice that the promise is to Caleb and his children, which directly applies to Caleb's daughter Aksah. After Othniel wins Aksah's hand in marriage (15:16–17), Caleb gives part of his inheritance to the newlyweds and he gives her a second parcel of the land when she requests for it (vv. 18–20).

Aksah's inheritance forms part of her dowry and remains in the family of Caleb and Othniel, and it witnesses to God's ongoing blessing for Caleb's faith.

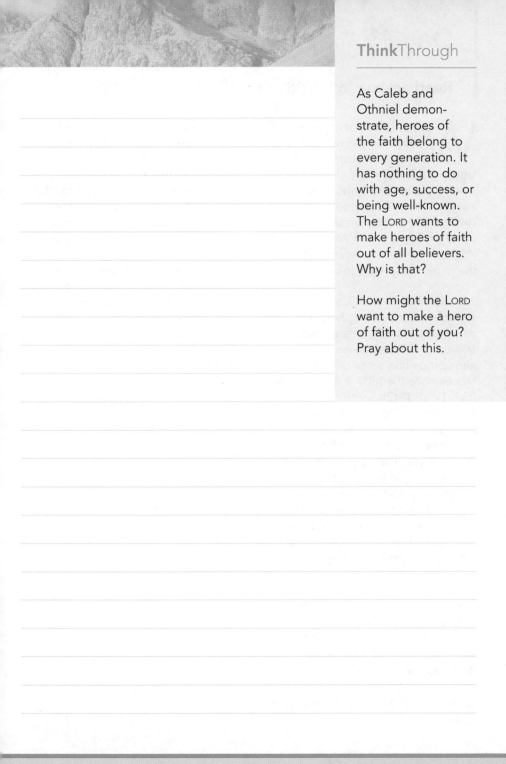

ThinkThrough

As Caleb and Othniel demonstrate, heroes of the faith belong to every generation. It has nothing to do with age, success, or being well-known. The LORD wants to make heroes of faith out of all believers. Why is that?

How might the LORD want to make a hero of faith out of you? Pray about this.

Day 19

Read Joshua 16:1–17:18

When several tribes do not drive out the remaining hostile inhabitants of the land, Joshua's plans to divide the land among the Israelite tribes starts to go awry. We saw this happen to Judah (Joshua 15:63), and we see it happen again to Ephraim and West Manasseh (16:10; 17:12–13, 16)—descendants of the mighty patriarch Joseph.

Joshua is happy to talk to the five women of faith—Zelophehad's daughters Mahlah, Noah, Hoglah, Milkah, and Tirzah—who clearly and compellingly cite the promise Moses gave them (17:4, see Numbers 27:1–11; 36:1–12). Some of the men may have baulked at assigning family lands to women, as traditionally, only sons inherited land from their fathers. Joshua may have felt pressured by them, but nevertheless, he appears glad to obey the LORD and implement an important legal precedent (Joshua 17:4). Women in that patriarchal society had limited rights, but now, they had one more.

In contrast, Joshua is not ready to entertain the leaders of Ephraim and West Manasseh, who bicker and complain about the size of their allotment (v. 14). When they complain that it is too small for their large population, Joshua challenges them to clear the trees and settle in the forested hill country (v. 15). But this is not what they want to hear. They insist that the hill country is not sufficient for them, and that the Canaanites in the region possess iron chariots (v. 16). Again, Joshua reminds his fellow tribesmen that they are numerous and powerful, and therefore fully capable of expanding their territory by clearing the hill country and driving out the enemy Canaanites (vv. 17–18).

If only they would exhibit courageous faith!

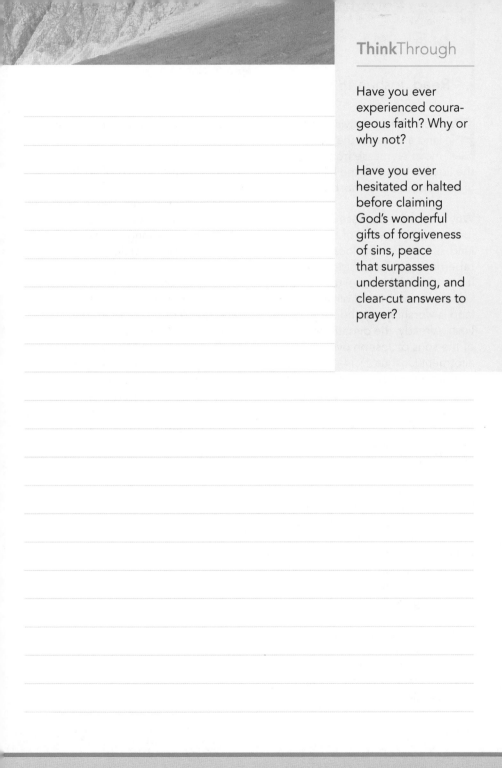

ThinkThrough

Have you ever experienced courageous faith? Why or why not?

Have you ever hesitated or halted before claiming God's wonderful gifts of forgiveness of sins, peace that surpasses understanding, and clear-cut answers to prayer?

Read Joshua 18:1–10

Before the final divisions of the land are made, the Israelites move en masse from Gilgal in the Jordan Valley to the hill country of Shiloh, about 30 km northwest.

Why? Probably because Shiloh, located at the centre of the promised land, is a convenient location for the tabernacle, or Tent of Meeting. Here, it can remind the Israelites that the key to prosperity and blessing in the land is worshipping and serving the LORD. Already, the dissatisfaction of the sons of Joseph over their allotment (Joshua 17:14–18) has given an ominous foreshadowing of the future disintegration of the nation over self-interest. To counteract this tendency, the tabernacle is set up in Shiloh to promote a sense of national unity (18:1).

Joshua is committed to dividing the rest of the land among the remaining seven tribes. The tribes aren't complaining like Ephraim or Manasseh, but they don't seem to be taking any action. They've done the waiting, but they haven't started the action to go with it (v. 3). So, Joshua organises them for action: he sends 21 men to survey the remaining regions, and with their report, he "then cast lots for them in Shiloh in the presence of the LORD, and there he distributed the land to the Israelites according to their tribal divisions" (v. 10).

Throughout the book of Joshua, Joshua hears the LORD God in a variety of ways. Sometimes, as in this case, he receives the LORD's will through the casting of lots. We will see this happen again later.

Of course, being assigned land is not the same as trusting the LORD and going on to conquer that land. Sadly, short-sighted self-interest and spiritual complacency go together. Oh, to be like Joshua and Caleb, who have worshipped and served the LORD wholeheartedly for a lifetime. What heroes of the faith, indeed!

What is your own experience of spiritual compla- cency? What do you think causes it?

In your experience, what can help you begin intentional actions that honour and glorify the LORD?

Read Joshua 18:11–19:9

After sending the 21 men to survey the remaining land and receiving their written report (Joshua 18:9), Joshua gathers the leaders of the tribes. He "then cast lots for them in Shiloh in the presence of the LORD, and there he distributed the land to the Israelites according to their tribal divisions" (v. 10). This distribution is for the seven tribes who are still awaiting their territorial assignments (18:11–20:9), plus the Levites (21:1–45).

The first two lots go to Benjamin and Simeon (18:11–20; 19:1–9). Their lands are tightly bound to those of Judah: Benjamin's territory rests atop Judah's, and Simeon's territory is within Judah's.

In later years, two or all three of these tribes will work closely together some of the time. In the book of Judges, Judah and Simeon will combine their might to fight the Canaanites (Judges 1:3, 17). And during King Rehoboam's reign, after the nation is divided, Judah and Benjamin will come together to war against the northern tribes of Israel (1 Kings 12:21–24).

At other times, Judah and Benjamin will find themselves competing fiercely against each other. This competition was seen during King Saul's reign, after his successor, David, was anointed. David came from the tribe of Judah, while King Saul came from the tribe of Benjamin. While David never tried to harm Saul, Saul repeatedly tried to kill David (1 Samuel 18, 19, 24, 26).

Besides King Saul, other notable descendants of Benjamin include Ehud (Judges 3:15), Esther (Esther 2:5–7), and the apostle Paul (Romans 11:1). The tribe of Simeon, however, produces no biblical heroes of faith.

Whether a tribe produces heroes or not, one thing remains true: God has no grandchildren. **Each generation, and each person within that generation, will have to answer this important question:** *Will I choose to love the LORD my God wholeheartedly now and for the rest of my days? Or, will I reject the LORD and choose to do whatever is right in my own eyes?*

ThinkThrough

In your family, who loves the LORD? Instead of just writing their names, you may want to use their family titles too— e.g., "grandfather", "father", etc. Give thanks to God for them, and pray for more to turn to Him.

How can the Christians in your family work together to support each other?

Day 22

Read Joshua 19:10–39

After apportioning land to the tribes of Benjamin and Simeon, Joshua assigns the northern lands to the tribes of Zebulun, Issachar, Asher, and Naphtali (Joshua 19:10–16, 17–23, 24–31, 32–39).

The most notable biblical villains from Issachar are King Baasha and his son Elah (1 Kings 15:27–16:14), while the most notable heroes from Naphtali and Asher are, respectively, Barak (Judges 4:6–9) and Anna (Luke 2:36–38). Anna "never left the temple but worshipped night and day, fasting and praying" (v. 37), as she and others were "looking forward to the redemption of Jerusalem" (v. 38). They were looking forward to the long-awaited light that Isaiah had prophesied would dawn over the lands of Zebulun and Naphtali (see Isaiah 9:1–2; Matthew 4:12–16).

When that long-awaited light, Jesus, began His ministry, He went to the local synagogue in Nazareth (Luke 4:18–19) and read from Isaiah 61:1–2:

> "The Spirit of the LORD is on me,
>   because he has anointed me
>   to proclaim good news to the
>   poor.
> He has sent me to proclaim
>   freedom for the prisoners
>   and recovery of sight for the
>   blind,

to set the oppressed free,
    to proclaim the year of the
        LORD's favour."

Unexpectedly, Jesus stopped reading mid-sentence. Even more unexpectedly, He then announced that "Today this scripture is fulfilled in your hearing" (Luke 4:21). In doing so, He was claiming to be the promised Messiah.

Today, many people think of Jesus as a good man. To be sure, Jesus "went around doing good" (Acts 10:38) during His three-year ministry. But, let's not mistake Him for being just a good man who did good works. When He healed the blind, He was not trying to be altruistic. And He was certainly not trying to be a better man. When Jesus came to earth, He came as the Messiah, and He fulfilled the prophecy made thousands of years ago by the prophet Isaiah.

Today, as we read about the allotment of lands to the tribes of Zebulun, Issachar, Asher, and Napthali, let's remember that God has fulfilled a greater promise than His promise to bring the Israelites to the promised land. He has come as the Light prophesied to dawn over the lands

of Zebulun and Naphtali to save His people from their sins!

ThinkThrough

Imagine being at the scene when Jesus and His family visited the temple, and Anna came forward to speak about Him (Luke 2:36–38). How do you think you might have felt? Why?

Reflect on who Jesus is. Turn your reflection into praise.

Day 23

Read Joshua 19:40–48

Last but not least, Joshua assigns territory to the tribe of Dan (Joshua 19:40–48).

The best-known hero from Dan is Samson, whose birth was more highly anticipated and celebrated than any other Israelite of that era (Judges 13). Samson's calling was to be an exemplary, holy Nazirite throughout his life (vv. 5, 7). He was a strong man with great potential, but he proved to be a womaniser and an undisciplined man who indulged himself freely and allowed himself to be controlled by his passions.

To avoid Samson's sinful ways, we need God's Word and His Holy Spirit, who will work in and through us. In that regard, I am reminded of another biblical hero from the tribe of Dan—Oholiab.

Oholiab is one of the two lead men whom the LORD used to design and build the tabernacle and its contents. Together with the other skilled workers, he and Bezalel made the ark of the covenant, the mercy seat, the golden lampstand, the altar for burnt offerings, and all the furniture, equipment, and clothing used in the tabernacle (Exodus 31:6–11; 35:34–36:2; 38:23). At every turn, what they made had deep spiritual significance: everything they built was used to honour and worship the LORD God. Oholiab reminds us of what we can do when we are filled with the Holy Spirit.

In Old Testament times, the Spirit was given only to a few, and Moses yearned for the day when the Spirit would be given to all of God's people (Numbers 11:29). That miracle began on the day of Pentecost (Acts 2). Since then, as Jesus promised, the Spirit has been dwelling in every true Christian (Romans 8:9).

Because the Holy Spirit lives in us, we are temples of the Holy Spirit, both collectively and individually (1 Corinthians 3:16–17; 6:19–20). This breathtaking truth calls us to live honourably and gracefully in all we say and do.

How have you been using your God-given ability to honour and glorify Him? How can you guard against squandering it away in sinful living?

How will you ask the Holy Spirit to empower you this coming week?

Day 24

Read Joshua 19:49–51

Just as they assigned land to Judah's hero, Caleb, the people now assign land to Ephraim's hero, Joshua (Joshua 14:6–15; 19:49–51). These two men are the only representatives of the previous generation who have remained faithful and who have entered the promised land to enjoy its blessings, as God promised (Numbers 14:30; 26:65; 32:12).

From serving as an assistant to his predecessor Moses in his youth, to his exploration of the promised land, Joshua has shown himself faithful in service, brave in battle, and mighty in faith. By faithfully and carefully obeying the LORD's orders in the Law of Moses as well as the LORD's orders revealed directly to him, Joshua has been able to lead the Israelites in conquering the promised land. In doing so, he has proved that all of God's great promises are trustworthy and true.

Joshua has always had the courage to obey the LORD God because he believes His promises wholeheartedly. That is why, when encouraging the Israelites—who have also seen all of God's promises come true—to take courage, he urges them to: "Be very strong; be careful to obey all that is written in the Book of the Law of Moses . . . hold fast to the LORD your God . . . be very careful to love the LORD your God" (Joshua 23:6–11).

If we find ourselves filled with fear, it might be because we have forgotten who the LORD God is and what He commands and promises in His Word. Like Joshua, we need to continually draw on our abiding source of courage. **Instead of counting on our own physical strength or mental abilities, we need to keep drawing on the presence and promises of the LORD God.**

All my worst moments in life—in my marriage, family, work, church, and community—have a common denominator: they took place when I forgot who the LORD God is and what He has commanded and promised in His Word.

My best moments in life also have a common denominator: they came when I made it a priority to write and pray words of thanksgiving to the LORD God for who He is, and to spend time each day in His Word. If you have come this far in *Journey Through Joshua*, you're doing exactly that. Keep at it!

Have you, like Joshua, been whole-hearted in obeying God? What needs to change so you could be considered a "good and faithful servant"?

What biblical words and phrases can you use to thank the LORD for who He is?

Day 25

Read Joshua 20:1–9

In the ancient world, blood revenge was widely practised. When a person was killed, his nearest relative took responsibility for vengeance. This rite of vendetta was often handed down from one generation to the next, with one act of revenge provoking another in turn. As a result, an increasing number of people died violently. This was why places of refuge were needed in ancient Israel.

After apportioning territory to all the tribes, Joshua now turns his focus to the LORD God's commands to designate six cities of refuge (Joshua 20:1–9). This careful distribution of cities throughout the nation of Israel ensures that anyone guilty of accidental manslaughter can flee to a city of refuge quickly.

Three of these cities lie west of the Jordan River, and form a fairly straight line north to south along a major trade route (v. 7). Kedesh is in the land of Naphtali, north of the Sea of Galilee; Shechem is in Ephraim; and Hebron is in Judah, west of the Dead Sea and south of Jerusalem.

The other three cities lie east of the Jordan River, and also follow another major trade route (v. 8). Bezer is in Reuben, east of the northern end of the Dead Sea, where the Jordan River ends; Ramoth is in Gad; and Golan is in East Manasseh, east of the southern end of the Sea of Galilee.

God is using these six cities of refuge to impress on Israel the sanctity of human life. To put an end to a person's life—even if unintentionally—is a serious thing, and the cities of refuge underscore this emphatically.

What's more, these cities of refuge also vividly illustrate the LORD's readiness to protect and forgive His people—including you and me. He did so ultimately through Jesus Christ's saving work on the cross for us and for our sins (Romans 5:8; 1 Corinthians 15:3; 1 Thessalonians 5:10; 1 Peter 2:24).

The LORD has done everything to forgive you for your sins. What is your response today?

What would it mean to honour the sanctity of human life today?

Read Joshua 21:1–45

n today's Scripture passage, Joshua converses with the leaders of the tribe of Levi (Joshua 21:1–2) and, following what Moses had commanded (Numbers 35:1–8), assigns the cities of refuge and 42 additional cities for them to share.

Of these, 10 cities lie east of the Jordan River within the lands of the tribes of East Manasseh, Reuben, and Gad (Joshua 21:27, 36–39). They zigzag from south (Kedemoth, south of Bezer) to north (Ashtaroth, north of Golan).

The other 38 cities lie west of the Jordan River. In the southern half of that region, 21 cities come from the tribes of Judah, Simeon, Benjamin, Ephraim, and Dan (vv. 9–24). In the northern half are 17 cities that come from the tribes of West Manasseh, Issachar, Asher, Naphtali, and Zebulun (vv. 25, 28–32, 34).

What's important about these Levitical cities is that they are shared, not exclusive. For instance, Bezer, a city of refuge, is inhabited by both Reubenites (20:8) and Levites (21:36).

Unlike other Israelite tribes, the Levites do not receive territory or cities for three primary reasons. First, their patriarch Jacob had said they would be "dispersed . . . in Israel" (Genesis 49:7). Second, the Levites serve the LORD and therefore receive the tithes of the other tribes (Numbers 18:21, 24; Deuteronomy 18:1; Joshua 13:14). Third, the LORD has said that He is their inheritance (Deuteronomy 10:9; Joshua 13:14, 33).

After the exodus from Egypt, Aaron served as the new nation's high priest for nearly four decades. Like his descendants, Aaron had days of incredible faith and obedience—and days of spectacular disbelief and disobedience. Other great biblical heroes from the tribe of Levi include Moses and Miriam; centuries later, Hilkiah and his grandson Ezra; and many centuries later, Elizabeth, Zachariah, and their son John the Baptist.

Don't miss the very last verse in today's Bible reading: "Not one of all the LORD's good promises to Israel failed; every one was fulfilled" (Joshua 21:45). If we believe this fully, we will have the courage and confidence to go through the toughest storms of life. And, when we fail, let's remember that we have a great High Priest in heaven, Jesus, who is able to "feel sympathy for our weaknesses" (Hebrews 4:14–15) and "is able to save completely those who come

to God through him, because he always lives to intercede for them" (7:25). What a Saviour!

Which of the LORD's good promises is your favourite? Why?

Which of the LORD's promises have been fulfilled in your own life? If so, how?

Day 27

Read Joshua 22:1–34

After the Levitical cities are assigned, Joshua commends the two-and-a-half eastern tribes, and grants them permission to return to their homes, east of the Jordan (Joshua 22:1–5). His words to them bear special attention.

In verse 4, Joshua says: "Now that the LORD your God has given them rest as he promised, return to your homes in the land that Moses the servant of the LORD gave you on the other side of the Jordan." This verse has a triple significance. First, it reaffirms the promises kept by the LORD. Second, it reaffirms the lands granted by Moses, God's representative. Third, it affirms the promises kept by the eastern tribes to help their fellow Israelites conquer the rest of the promised land.

In verse 5, Joshua adds: "But be very careful to keep the commandment and the law that Moses the servant of the LORD gave you: to love the LORD your God, to walk in obedience to him, to keep his commands, to hold fast to him and to serve him with all your heart and with all your soul." I believe this is one of the key verses in this book (the other being 24:15).

Each of Joshua's five challenges applies to you and me today.

First, we are to read and keep God's Word.

Second, we are to love the LORD our God.

Third, we are to obey all of His commands. In this regard, Joshua himself is a stellar example.

Fourth, like Joshua, we are to hold fast to the LORD. Our journey of faith is to be a lifelong commitment to finish well in the LORD's eyes.

Fifth, we are to serve the LORD wholeheartedly. Serving God can be done in three ways: wholeheartedly, half-heartedly, or no-heartedly. Only the first brings blessing, the second is unsustainable, and the third will only end in disaster.

After Joshua's stirring challenge, the eastern tribes head home (22:6–9). Their actions and allegiance are soon questioned, however, and civil war is narrowly averted—thanks to Phinehas (vv. 10–33). How good that Phinehas listened to the facts and was willing to change his mind.

Why the focus on Aaron's grandson Phinehas? Like Moses and Joshua, Phinehas is a servant of the LORD, ready to do whatever the LORD

commands. As a result, it "was credited to him as righteousness for endless generations to come" (Psalm 106:31). Like Joshua and Phinehas, may we always be ready do what the LORD commands!

Which of Joshua's five challenges resonates with you the most? Why?

Which of Joshua's challenges is the hardest for you? Why?

Day 28

Read Joshua 23:1–16

Even though he is about 110 years old by now, Joshua is not finished yet. To Joshua, nothing is more important than finishing well. To finish well includes carefully passing the baton to the next generation, in spoken word and written form.

In this chapter, Joshua begins the process of passing the baton by delivering a farewell address to the Israelite leaders (Joshua 23:2–16). He exhorts them to remain true to the LORD, just as the LORD has remained true to them (vv. 6–11). In essence, he is challenging them: Be strong. Obey God's Law. Remember that the LORD is with you to fight for you!

Don't miss the phrase, "to this day" (v. 9). This is the 12th time this particular phrase is being used in the book of Joshua—far more often than in any other book of the Bible. It confirms that this truth (that no-one can withstand Israel) is still the case for generations of Israelites who unlike soldiers and nomads, typically stayed close to home year in and year out. Even though they have never travelled to the river Jordan (4:9), city of Gilgal (5:9), Valley of Achor (7:26), Ai (8:28–29), cave at Makkedah (10:27), cities of Geshur and Maakah (13:13), or city of Gezer (16:10), and let alone travelled to meet Rahab (6:25) or the Gibeonites (9:27), they continue to experience the protection and presence of God, just as their forefathers did, in the accounts that they've heard in the book of Joshua.

Also, don't miss 23:14–15, which encapsulate two of Joshua's most important themes. Listen to what he says first: "You know with all your heart and soul that not one of all the good promises the LORD your God gave you has failed. Every promise has been fulfilled; not one has failed" (v. 14).

Then again: "But just as all the good things the LORD your God has promised you have come to you, so he will bring on you all the evil things he has threatened, until the LORD your God has destroyed you from this good land he has given you" (v. 15).

The choice to believe and claim God's promises is theirs, and now it is ours, too. May you and I seek the LORD God's very best!

How can you finish well in your walk with God? What habits do you need to cultivate? What examples of faith would you like to leave behind for those after you?

Which of God's promises will you claim today?

Day 29

Read Joshua 24:1–28

After addressing the Israelite leaders, Joshua travels to Shechem (Joshua 24:1). There, he delivers his farewell address to members of every Israelite tribe. Once again, he exhorts them to remain true to the LORD, just as the LORD had remained true to them.

In his speech, Joshua quotes the LORD (vv. 2–13). Don't miss verse 7, where the LORD says: "You saw with your own eyes what I did to the Egyptians." The "you" here is a collective second-person plural that refers to *some*—not all—of the people. More specifically, it refers to those aged 75 and older, a number of whom are revered leaders (see v. 31). Similarly, have you witnessed God's deliverance before? Have you seen His judgment on others? Do not forget them, so that you may continue to "fear the LORD and serve him with all faithfulness" (v. 14).

And as we have seen, the book of Joshua records only half a dozen occasions when people speak to Joshua directly. The second half of today's Bible reading is one of those occasions, and is the most dramatic. If you are reading this with a family member or friend, take turns to read the passage aloud. Give special emphasis to these famous and stirring words: "But as for me and my household, we will serve the LORD" (v. 15).

Right before this key verse, and again in verse 23, Joshua exhorts the people to rid themselves of idols and foreign gods. Essentially, he is echoing what the patriarch Jacob had said to his household in Genesis 35:2—"Get rid of the foreign gods you have with you, and purify yourselves." Moses and many other Old Testament heroes of the faith had said the same thing. What's more, this theme carries over into the New Testament—in book of Acts, in the epistles, and in the book of Revelation. **Idols and false gods have no place in the life of Christians who know, believe, and trust the one true LORD God.** It's time to make a clean break with the past!

Also, don't miss Joshua's important last words to the people in Joshua 24:27. In essence, he says: "Keep your word. Do not break your promises to the LORD God, or you will suffer needlessly." His words foreshadow a millennium and a half of Israel's history. Thankfully, Joshua's last words—"it will be a witness against you if you are untrue to your God"—do not have to foreshadow our own future. Instead, may you and I carefully love, trust, obey, and serve the LORD faithfully all of our days!

_____

_____

_____

_____

_____

_____

How can you and your household serve the LORD? What are some idols that you need to get rid of?

How can you ensure that you will love, trust, obey, and serve the LORD faithfully all of your days? Think of three ways that will help you.

Read Joshua 24:29–33

This wonderful book about God's promises ends with a brief appendix. This appendix affirms Joshua's legacy as he dies at the ripe old age of 110 and receives an honourable burial on his own land (Joshua 24:29–30). Just as Joshua had repeatedly described Moses as "the servant of the LORD", after his own death Joshua, too, is called "the servant of the LORD" (v. 29). What a fitting epitaph!

The appendix also tells us about the burial of two other servants of the LORD—the great patriarch Joseph (v. 32; see Genesis 50:24–25; Exodus 13:19; Hebrews 11:22); and Eleazar, son of Aaron, who took over the role of high priest after Aaron passed away (v. 33; see Numbers 20:25–28; Deuteronomy 10:6). Eleazar's final role was overseeing Israel's allotment (Joshua 14:1; 17:4; 19:51; 21:1).

What has the book of Joshua taught us? Four enduring truths stand head and shoulders above the rest.

First, even the strongest men and women need to take courage. This is clearly seen in Joshua's life. From his clandestine exploration of the promised land to his service for 40 years alongside Moses, Joshua has shown himself to be faithful in service, brave in battle, and mighty in faith.

Second, the LORD gladly saves you and me, no matter our nationality, family background, or past. What's more, He rewards the faith of all who diligently seek Him (Hebrews 11:6). Rahab is proof that the LORD can make anyone a hero of faith. Now, He wants to do the same with our lives.

Third, the LORD's commands are often counterintuitive and His promises often seem humanly impossible. Yet, Joshua knows, trusts, believes, and immediately obeys. Like Joshua, may you and I do the same.

Finally, like Joshua, we need to continually draw on our abiding source of courage. That's not our own physical strength or mental abilities; rather, as Joshua has proved, it is the presence and promises of the LORD God almighty. **How good that you and I can be filled with courage daily because of God's exceedingly great promises to us!**

In the end, does Joshua fulfil the LORD God's purposes in his generation? Without a doubt, yes. Does the LORD keep all of His promises to Joshua? Again, yes. How good that we can thank the LORD daily for His promise-keeping mercy, grace, and love for us!

Rewrite this prayer in your own words: "LORD, You know the number of my days. May I bring You glory, honour, and praise."

After journeying through the book of Joshua, what do you most remember? What will you put into practice?

Going Deeper
in Your Walk
with Christ

Whether you're a new Christian or have been
a Christian for a while, it's worth taking a journey
through the Bible, book by book, to gain a deeper
appreciation of who Jesus is and how we can
follow Him.

Let faithful Bible teachers be your tour guides and
help you draw closer to Christ as you spend time
reading and reflecting on His Word.

Journey Through

Amos

The book of Amos contains some hard messages that their original listeners would have found difficult to swallow. Yet, amid the unrelenting warnings of judgment, we can find assurances of God's love and compassion. Journey through Amos, and discover how the strident call to repentance comes with the comforting promise of restoration.

J.R. Hudberg and his wife, Heidi, live in Grand Rapids, Michigan, with their two young boys. He was born in Grand Rapids and attended college in Canada (where he met Heidi). After spending time in Ohio, Montana, and California, he returned "home". In the garden, on a boat, or in the woods, J.R. spends as much time as he can with family and friends enjoying God's creation. He is the executive editor for Our Daily Bread Ministries' *Discovery Series* booklets and is a regular contributor to the Insights for *Our Daily Bread*.

Journey Through

Hosea

by David Gibb

As God's spokesman, Hosea is told by Him to marry Gomer, a prostitute, and to go again and again to woo her back despite her many infidelities. Hosea's commitment to love Gomer gives us a glimpse of God's love for us. God loves His people as passionately and as jealously as a devoted husband loves his wife. Even when we wander from Him and our hearts cool towards Him, He continues to come after us and to draw us back to Him. God's love will never let us go. Rekindle your love and commitment to the One who loves you!

David Gibb is the former Vicar of St. Andrew's Church in Leyland and Honorary Canon of Blackburn Cathedral. He is committed to training church planters and gospel workers, and is one of the contributors to a new NIV Study Bible. He is also author of a book on Revelation.

Journey Through
Judges

by David Inrig

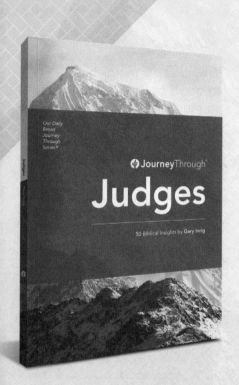

The book of Judges describes a low point in the history of God's people. It tells of a time of moral and spiritual anarchy, when everyone ignored God's life-giving laws and did what they thought was right in their own eyes. It is a story of disobedience and defeat. Yet the book also contains glimpses of the Israelites' capacity for greatness—when they chose to trust and depend on God. Discover God's great principles of life, and find out how we can lead powerful, productive lives in a society that is increasingly hostile to our faith.

Gary Inrig is a graduate of the University of British Columbia and Dallas Theological Seminary. An established Bible teacher and former pastor, he has authored several books, including *True North*, *The Parables*, *Forgiveness*, and *Whole Marriages in a Broken World*.

Journey Through

Job

Why do bad things happen to good people? Why is there so much seemingly senseless suffering? Many of us are still asking these questions that plagued Job, a real believer who suffered great loss and experienced agony and abandonment, and who foreshadows Jesus Christ so deeply. Explore these difficult questions as you journey through Job, and discover how you can renew your hope and trust in an all-powerful God who holds us in His loving care.

Christopher Ash is Writer-in-Residence at Tyndale House, Cambridge, England. He is the author of a full-length commentary on Job, *Job: the Wisdom of the Cross* and a brief introduction, *Trusting God in the Darkness*.

Journey Through with your
Bible study group!

Many of our *Journey Through* books now come with group
Bible study lessons. All our lessons include printable handouts
and lesson plans, which are free for you to use. And several have
video contributions as well. Why not *Journey Through* with your
Bible study group at **ourdailybread.org/studies**

Browse and purchase all our available *Journey Through* Series
books at **ourdailybreadpublishing.org.uk/journey-through**

For information on our resources, visit **ourdailybread.org**. Alternatively, please contact the office nearest you from the list below, or go to **ourdailybread.org/locations** for the complete list of offices.

BELARUS
Our Daily Bread Ministries
PO Box 82, Minsk, Belarus 220107
belarus@odb.org • (375-17) 2854657; (375-29) 9168799

GERMANY
Our Daily Bread Ministries e.V.
Schulstraße 42, 79540 Lörrach
deutsch@odb.org • +49 (0) 7621 9511135

IRELAND
Our Daily Bread Ministries
64 Baggot Street Lower, Dublin 2, D02 XC62
ireland@odb.org • +353 (0) 1676 7315

RUSSIA
MISSION Our Daily Bread
PO Box "Our Daily Bread",
str.Vokzalnaya 2, Smolensk, Russia 214961
russia@odb.org • 8(4812)660849; +7(951)7028049

UKRAINE
Christian Mission Our Daily Bread
PO Box 533, Kiev, Ukraine 01004
ukraine@odb.org • +380964407374; +380632112446

UNITED KINGDOM (Europe Regional Office)
Our Daily Bread Ministries
PO Box 1, Millhead, Carnforth, LA5 9ES
europe@odb.org • +44 (0)15395 64149

ourdailybread.org